WARRIOR REBORN

The Extraordinary True Story of Kisemei Kupe

An official narrative biography
from transcripts by Stephanie Wiginton
written by Clark Wiginton

CLAY BRIDGES
P R E S S

Warrior Reborn
The Extraordinary True Story of Kisemei Kupe
Copyright © 2023 by Clark Wiginton

Published by Clay Bridges Press in Houston, TX
www.ClayBridgesPress.com

ISBN: 978-1-68488-060-7
eISBN: 978-1-68488-059-1

Special Sales: Most Clay Bridges titles are available in special quantity discounts. Custom imprinting or excerpting can also be done to fit special needs. Contact Clay Bridges at Info@ClayBridgesPress.com

This book is dedicated to the glory of God and to everyone who needs to hear that biblical-scale miracles still happen today.

Special Thanks

I extend very special thanks to Kisemei Kupe. It is an honor to share his story with the world.

I would also like to extend a very heartfelt thanks to my wife, Stephanie Wiginton, for the many hours she spent preparing and editing the transcripts of our interviews with Kisemei and for her relentless patience and commitment to the making of this book. I will always owe her a debt of gratitude. Stephanie, I love you forever.

Contents

Preface

It was a Sunday like any other, yet in the course of the morning, I would meet a man with a story that would leave a lasting impression on my life.

His name was Kisemei Kupe. He came to visit our study group and briefly share his life story. It was a condensed testimony that abbreviated and omitted many of the moments he had experienced. Yet even in this short, simple, hour-long format, it was a testimony that quickly turned the mood of our casual, chatty group of friends into a humble assembly of silent, captivated onlookers.

Born into obscurity, poverty, and indifference in the 1960s in the heart of the African continent, Kisemei encountered neglect, loneliness, hunger, abuse, misdirection, and danger to a degree that very few who are raised in Western culture could imagine. And little could anyone from any background imagine the dramatic, true circumstances through which he was saved from his predicament. Physically and forcefully yanked from the jaws of seemingly inevitable ruin, Kisemei encountered an inescapable force that intervened in his life—a force so undeniable, so extraordinarily personified in Kisemei's story that it is a force we must conclude is none other than the presence of God himself.

In our time, it seems that humanity is rife with stories of tragedy, failure, death, destruction, and extinction. To compensate, we often invent stories of fantasy and fill them with positivity to escape from reality or to fabricate augmented moments of happiness in our lives.

Yet even in times of sorrow, there are still positive, true stories to be found. There are true accounts of the active, intervening hand of God in our modern world. Such true stories bolster our hope and strength far beyond the capacity of any well-versed fantasy. We long to hear such good news—to be uplifted by positive facts. We long for accounts of God actively at work in our age. We are hungry for these stories. We need to hear these true tales of hope.

To Kisemei, his metamorphosis was so genuine, so dramatic, and so undeniably positive that he was willing to face certain death to follow the new life he found. It is a story that many of us need to hear—a story that transcends the scrutiny of the jury of society, an abiding story of truth and hope for us all. Such a transformation deserves to be preserved for posterity.

After meeting Kisemei that morning, I could not find peace until I resolved that the life he had lived—this particular true story of one extraordinary life—would be preserved and retold. It was then that I decided to put to paper everything Kisemei would share with me over the next few months.

This is the true story of Kisemei Kupe.

CHAPTER I

A Baby in a Distant Land

It was a still night. The silent stars were like a glowing cloud assembled in a row with the wispy twinkling of a billion suns. Far below in a village perched low on the northeastern slope of the mighty, snow-capped Kilimanjaro stood a small, domed, earthen dwelling. The Chyulu Hills stood guard on the northeastern horizon as the faint sound of shuffling cattle in the distance drifted and mingled with odors of woody smoke and cow dung in the cool morning air. Kupe Lenkujuk paced slowly outside the doorway of his home, his sandals carving at the fine, red dirt that powdered his toes. A warm light filled his earth-dung-and-straw home just beyond the hide that hung above the house's threshold.

With a degree of cold repose, Kupe called out in his native Maa language, "What is going on in there?"

There was no answer. The one-room, earthen home that Leah had built for her new family was awash with commotion and chattering between the midwife and a neighbor among the sounds of labor. Kupe listened and asked again impatiently, "Is she okay?" He was now more concerned. His wife, Leah, had been sick for the last month of her pregnancy, a malady for which she had blamed her unborn child. The midwife thought the child may not survive. Leah was now significantly past due. The midwife had pressed on Leah's chest and abdomen off and on throughout the previous day to induce labor. Kupe paced along the outside perimeter of his home as the commotion inside grew to a fervor.

Then through the single, small window at the side of the rectangular house rose the sound of a weak, small cry, but still more time elapsed with no report. Kupe strained for a glimpse through the small, open-air window at the front of the house just as the midwife thrust her head out the doorway. "She has been bleeding heavily but I think she will be okay. Come and see your child."

As Kupe entered the home, he saw his wife resting on the straw bedding on the dirt floor and covered in a brightly colored crimson blanket. She looked up at him with a weary smile. "Come and meet your son, Kupe," she said quietly.

Kupe stood tall. A broad grin spread across his face as he looked on while the midwife cleaned and wrapped the child. "A son, Leah! You have given me a son!"

Interrupting his jubilance, Leah weakly sighed, "Yes, Kupe" as the midwife laid the baby beside her. Leaning over, Kupe cautiously gazed into the face of the child, carefully studying each subtle nuance of his new, moist face.

"Would you like to hold him?" Leah asked.

Kupe slowly brought the bundle of brightly colored cloth and child to his chest. "His name will be Kisemei—Kisemei Kupe. Someday he will be a mighty Maasai warrior," he whispered.

Leah smiled with pride and gently added, "Yes, a warrior. Not like his father." Kupe turned and frowned an unsettling glare at Leah. Everyone in the room knew exactly what she meant. They knew Kupe very well. And soon Kisemei would come to know his father as others did. It would become a relationship of heartbreaking pain. But for tonight at least, Leah's baby breathed the dusty air in peace.

CHAPTER II

The Maasai

As the golden sun rose that morning, the mighty, snow-capped, monolithic Kilimanjaro sat high on the southwestern horizon, glowing in the morning sunlight as the Chyulu Hills cast a broad, dim shadow across the valley east of the Maasai village. The men rose to tend to the cattle while the children scurried among the huts. Villagers began to gather to meet the newest member of the Maasai tribe.

Tall, slender, and clad in brightly woven crimson garments, the Maasai stood shoulders above the other tribes of the region. They attributed the trait to the distant origins of their people of whom their elders spoke from ancient oral tradition.

On Mount Suswa east of the city of Nairobi, the Maasai traveled to consult their elders who retold their ancient oral history passed down to them from countless generations before. Their legends were long-cherished traditions preserved in the memories of the oldest members of the Maasai villages. These tales of old spanned the boundaries of eons and kingdoms and told of their countless journeys from long ago. Nomadic for thousands of years, the Maasai had legends that described their origins in the wilderness of Egypt and other parts of North Africa and onward to Ethiopia and Sudan. Eventually, many generations ago, the Maasai arrived at a vast, fertile land spanning onward as eternally as the horizon, teeming with birds, wild beasts, and vegetation, crowned by a mighty lone mountain now called Kilimanjaro. Legend was that when the Maasai arrived in this area, now known as the Rift Valley, they carried a sacred scroll from their ancestors. They soaked the scroll in oil, wrapped it in sheepskin, and buried it for posterity. It is there in this majestic landscape that they remained for as long as written history records, immersed in a realm of tribal unity and mysticism, shunning the tides of change around them.

But as time progressed, an era of hardship unfolded for the Maasai. At the end of the 19th century, a plague called the Emutai, or the wipeout, claimed up to half of the indigenous wildlife. By that time, the Maasai had begun also to rely heavily on cattle, both as a means of sustenance and as currency. The dreaded Emutai mercilessly claimed up to 90 percent of their cattle. Amid this fearsome pestilence, a year-long drought scourged the earth beneath the Maasai. The toll was a heavy one to bear. Two-thirds of their people's men, women, and children perished.

Soon, the passing foreign tribes began to give way to strange, pale people with peculiar languages and metal weaponry. These new intruders were sparse at first but increased with time, bringing with them the ways of the continent of Europe and establishing colonies with European laws, languages, and infrastructure in the African plains. As the powers of Europe vied to establish colonies in the great southern continent beyond the Mediterranean, the surviving members of the Maasai fiercely defended their tribal bands and villages throughout the region, holding fast to their traditions and shunning outsiders with pride and fury. But the Maasai weaponry, mostly consisting of spears and stone knives, was no match for late 19th-century European firepower, and many more Maasai lost their lives in the throes of battle.

As the decades of the late 19th and early to mid-20th centuries unfolded, the world around the Maasai grew ever smaller while the pervasive European colonies evolved into modern, independent African nations. By then, the formerly vast herding grounds of the mighty Maasai became little more than a vestige of their former grandeur as the tribe and its villages became surrounded by encroaching plantations, ranches, cities, and roadways. The colonial British population had forced the Maasai from their most fertile herding grounds, leaving the tribe to subsist on the arid plains at the edge of their once vast territories in Kenya and Tanzania.

Nevertheless, by the 1920s, regional principalities and national governments grew to respect the Maasai for their staunch adherence to culture and traditions that time had elsewhere long since abandoned.

In 1927, the Kenyan government declared the remaining lands of the Maasai a closed district and set them aside as reserves where the tribe could live in peace in their ancestral homeland, independent of the governance of national powers. They were left to live, govern, worship, and die on their own terms under the traditions of their ancient ways. The Tanzanian government soon followed suit, but the Maasai had given up their most fertile lands a generation before and now found themselves subsisting in a baseline state of poverty in the dusty sub-arid plains at the base of Kilimanjaro.

And as history retells time and time again, governmental promises made in perpetuity are easier to author than to practice. With the encroachment of wealthy foreign landowners, huge swaths of land just beyond the Maasai reserves became tamed and reclaimed by outsiders. The wandering herds of elephant and African buffalo were substituted with private herds of cattle. The mighty, iconic beasts of the African plains grew scarce as an incessant procession of hunters and poachers extinguished countless lions, elephants, and smaller game bound for the taxidermists of the Western world. The animals upon which the Maasai had thrived for countless generations became an uncommon prize rather than a staple of life.

So too came encroachments on the Maasai culture. Curious travelers began to venture into Maasai territory to gawk at the mysterious tribe that had by then attained considerable renown in distant Western lands. Poachers stole natural resources as they pleased. The Maasai people were exposed to the good and the bad of foreign humanity in all its frank reality.

CHAPTER III

A Broken Home and Alone

It was in this world of change, turmoil, and uncertainty that Kisemei awoke that day, his first morning. Despite the shortcomings of human efforts, the sun still faithfully rose just as before, shining its warmth into the vast valley at the base of Kilimanjaro, the same as it had for untold time before.

Yet below the sun, in the Olgirra Clan village of the Maasai, turmoil permeated even the walls of Kupe's small, earthen home that Leah had built. Leah's health continued to falter after the birth of her son. Just as she had before his birth, Leah continued to foster a sense of distance toward her young son, ultimately a product of the pregnancy complications that continued to haunt her. With time, this distance forged a mild degree of perpetual resentment between mother and child and between father and son. Kisemei was just another villager to them, another inconvenience, another mouth to feed among the ever-present, relentless struggle of village life. He was such an inconvenience that his parents could not justify the effort to record Kisemei's early life events, and even the calendar date and year of his birth would remain unknown.

Nevertheless, when Kisemei was three months old, the tribe held a ceremony in the village for Kupe and Leah's child. They sacrificed a lamb and shaved Kupe's son's head. It was the traditional naming ceremony, a ritual bestowed upon all Maasai boys fortunate enough to survive the high rate of infant mortality. At the ceremony, Kupe officially named his son Kisemei.

Within a short time, Kupe grew tired of Leah. As was common in Maasai culture, Kupe had children from other women before her. A cyclical pattern of discontent began to revolve again in Kupe's heart. Anger and strife gave way to aggression and violence. Kupe became cruel to Leah, and soon rumors of these troubles reached the ears of Kupe's adoptive father, Lenkujuk Ntigoyo.

But Kupe's bitterness extended beyond the boundaries of his home. He was born into a Maasai village in Merrueshi, Kenya, and his birth parents gave him away at an early age. Kupe moved far across the Kenyan plains to live with his cousin Lenkujuk Ntigoyo's family. Lenkujuk's wife could not bear a son of her own. As was common in many cultures, a male was a valuable asset to a Maasai family since he provided an heir. Lenkujuk took Kupe into his home and raised him as his own son. In the Maasai culture, a man's last name was taken from the first name of his father, so in keeping with tradition, Kupe was given Lenkujuk's name as his own, becoming Kupe Lenkujuk. His new father, Lenkujuk Ntigoyo, had grown wealthy in his later years, amassing a herd of 7,000 cattle, along with sheep, goats, and several parcels of land. But when Kupe was young, he was found to be irresponsible in the eyes of his adoptive father, and they argued often. Eventually, arguments gave way to anger, which matured into a bitter rivalry between father and son.

After Kupe married Leah, his hostility toward her eventually became so brutally violent that Leah was experiencing seizures from her head injuries. One morning when Kisemei was six months old, Leah was consumed with convulsions and fell head-first into the open fire in her house. Unable to remove herself from the flames, the commotion frightened her young infant son, Kisemei, who began to scream for his mother. Thankfully, Leah's mother-in-law heard the urgent screams and ran to investigate. She gasped in horror at the sight before her and quickly pulled her young daughter-in-law from the fire. Kisemei's mother survived the ordeal, although she was badly burned and carried permanent scars on her face for the rest of her life. When Lenkujuk heard what had happened, he became incensed with Kupe's abuse toward Leah. He came to Kupe's village with strong words for his son.

"This cruelty cannot continue!" he roared. "This violence and abuse are shameful to me and my household. You must separate from Leah. Kisemei will live with me."

"Oh, my baby!" cried Leah. The relief of impending reprieve from Kupe's abuse was instantly overshadowed by what she knew would inevitably cause her to lose her young son.

Though initially indifferent to her baby, the natural bond between mother and child had grown strong over the few months since Kisemei's birth. Leah loved her son and had always shielded him from the relentless cruelty of his father. Yet even though she loved and protected him as much as she could, Maasai law held that in the circumstance of separation or divorce, the father or the father's family was always awarded custody of the children. The mother always lost custody of her children regardless of the circumstances. The dowry could not be repaid nor could the children be returned to the wife or the wife's family.

Kisemei was the only legitimate child born to both his parents, but now his life was upended before he was old enough to grasp any of the events unfolding around him.

It was shameful to Lenkujuk that he had not produced an heir who was responsible enough to even raise his own grandson. Although he was by then quite elderly with failing health, he took Kisemei into his home to raise the boy as his own. And so it was that before Kisemei had celebrated his first birthday, he, like his father, was taken to the home of his adoptive grandparents for care. But Kisemei would later recall that those days living with his grandparents were the happiest childhood memories he would ever know.

We might expect that these events would ensure that Kisemei would mature under the roof of a nurturing stable home, but it was not to be. In a short while, time took its toll on Kisemei's loving, elderly family. Both of his grandparents soon died, and Kisemei found himself like an orphan. His father had remarried before he was legally divorced from Leah and before Kisemei was even two years old. Soon Kisemei found himself under the care of his new stepmother.

As the years passed, Kisemei's painful loneliness grew like thorns in his heart. His stepmother was cold and cruel, and his father was abusive and usually absent. Never taking a moment to nurture or raise Kisemei, they often would not even feed him. He regularly had to fend for himself, finding sustenance by squeezing milk directly into his mouth from a cow or taking corn from another family's crops to roast by himself over an outdoor fire or eat raw. Kisemei would later recall that during those times, he ate like the wild creatures of Africa. By then his family had lost the entirety of their worldly possessions. The comfortable life afforded by the wealth of his grandparents was now gone. He was alone within his own home.

Perhaps because of Kupe's hatred toward his wealthy, adopted father or perhaps just as much because of his utter lack of discretion or restraint, Kupe had squandered Lenkujuk's fortune as soon as he had inherited it. In fact, he began selling his father's cattle even before his father died, which was considered an egregiously shameful breach of tradition among the Maasai. But after Lenkujuk's death, the sale of his possessions happened quickly. Kupe would leave for months at a time, selling several hundred bulls with each excursion and in turn squandering the money on alcohol. The herds of livestock that remained behind were neglected. In a society where wealth was often measured in cattle rather than any form of physical money, Kupe's ranch hands saw this lack of oversight as an opportunity for themselves, and they occasionally stole cattle for food or extra money. As it became clear that this pattern showed no sign of reprieve, this neglect occasionally allowed Kupe's wife to take advantage of the opportunity to hide a calf from her husband at neighbors' homes as a way to save something for her family. But eventually, Kupe discovered these few cattle and sold them for money he ultimately squandered. Kupe and his wife soon found themselves utterly destitute. Once the unworthy proprietor of a vast fortune, Kupe was now reduced to wandering from location to location, finding work as a laborer at other landowners' farms.

One morning when Kisemei was no more than four or five years old, his stepmother pulled him aside. "I can't let you stay with us any longer," she coldly announced. Kisemei gazed up into her eyes, hoping to catch her glance. Crushed with fear, he pleaded, "But Mama, where will I go?"

Undeterred, she blankly stared down. "Your father and I have already decided. We cannot afford to feed you. I have to work in the fields alongside your father all day just so we can afford to eat. I cannot feed you too. And then when I get home I have so much else to do. I do not have time to raise a . . ."

". . . But Mama!" Kisemei interrupted, quivering as he clung to her, his bare feet shifting under his small, tender frame. "I can feed myself. I already do. Just let me sleep in the house. I can stay away the rest of the time. We have a house."

In cases of destitution, the Maasai tradition incorporated a system designed to provide for members of the tribe. They had provided Kupe and his wife with a place to live, but they owned nothing.

"It's for us, Kisemei, not you," scolded his stepmother. "We can't take care of you. It has already been arranged. We will take you to your cousin's house and leave you there."

So before Kisemei was old enough to attend school, he found himself passed from household to household, sometimes with his father's cousins and sometimes with his stepmother's family. His parents had once deprived their son of food and nurturing, but now Kisemei was deprived of even the assurance of a stable place to sleep. He was once again like an orphan among his own family.

But such a life was still better than the perils that awaited him just around the corner.

CHAPTER IV

Slavery

One dry, windy evening, Kisemei was playing in a field near his step-mother's relatives' house. As the sun began to set, illuminating the snow-capped crown of Kilimanjaro in the distance, Kisemei heard the grinding crackle of car tires and saw a trail of grayish-red dust approaching in the distance. He rose to his feet as a Land Rover came into view beyond the bushy brush near the house. The truck approached at a rapid pace. Kisemei's stepmother was at the residence that evening and noticed the approaching vehicle. She rushed outside, grabbed Kisemei, and watched as the truck approached.

Bewildered, Kisemei stared forward in confusion as the Land Rover sped to the front of the house and slid to a stop. Both doors were now thrown open.

"It's about time!" she called out to the approaching visitors. "What took you so long?"

Two large men leaped from the truck and stomped straight toward the boy as he braced against his stepmother. "No! Leave me alone," Kisemei yelled as screaming erupted from the on-looking family members near the house.

"Kisemei clung tenderly to his stepmother's shuka. Looking up at her longingly, he begged, "Mama, I don't want to go with these men." He held firmly to her, but it was to no avail.

His stepmother coldly pried the young boy's hands loose from the hem of her shuka and nudged him forward toward the approaching strangers.

"Go with them," she ordered as she shoved the boy awkwardly. Kisemei looked up at her with immeasurable fright. "No, Mama!"

She shoved him more forcefully forward as the men grasped at Kisemei's arms. "Go, go, go," she said coldly through a smile. The two men seized the small child and forcefully jerked him from his grasp on his stepmother.

"No!" Kisemei screamed over and over as he flailed and kicked with all his boyish might. The two men effortlessly overpowered him. "Quiet!" one of them howled as the men began to beat the child with blow after blow. They beat Kisemei until he gave up his struggle and reduced his shouts to sobbing. The men dragged the boy to the Land Rover and shoved him between them in the front seat.

"Go!" the passenger barked to the driver. The tires swirled in the red dust as the Land Rover flung an about-face and lurched away over the dusty road and out of sight.

The writhing sobs of the terrified young boy were drowned by the engine and gearbox of the loud, rattling bush truck as it whined and strained at full speed, the suspension rumbling, slamming, and bumping its way across the African plain. Kisemei's face was glossed with a river of muddy tears, unwiped by his bound hands. The large, burly passenger held a crushing grip on Kisemei as the driver wrestled with the large, narrow steering wheel. The two men glared at the road ahead of them, glancing down at Kisemei only occasionally to check the status of their young cargo.

After what seemed like an eternity to the boy, the rapid advance and frantic noise of the Land Rover began to diminish. Kisemei sat up and craned his neck to capture a glimpse of the path ahead. They approached the gate to a farm. In the distance was a substantially large, stone ranch house. Kisemei could see the figure of a Maasai woman sitting on the porch. As the house came into full view through the dust-smeared windshield, the woman rose to her feet and paced slowly to the road. Much more calmly than their previous exit, the two men opened the doors and, holding tightly to Kisemei, walked him up next to the woman.

With a slow, slight smile, the woman examined the boy, extending his arms and scanning him from bottom to top. Then leaning over, she forced her slight smile slightly wider. "What is your name?" she quietly asked in Maa.

Timidly, still sobbing, and with dust caked in his drying tears, the boy managed to struggle through his name, his lungs and neck jerking with sobs as he spoke. "Ki-Kisemei," he said.

"Well, Kisemei," answered the woman. "Welcome to your new home."

Kisemei was quite accustomed to the process of being regularly relocated to different residences but never one like this and never with such brutality and force. He could still feel a frail, battered glimmer of hope rising in his heart, but none of the cruel turmoil thrust into his young life by the adults around him could prepare him for what he heard next.

The woman turned to pace slowly toward the porch as she spoke, motioning for Kisemei to follow her. "My husband is gone," she explained. "I'm a widow. And I need help tending to this ranch and my home. My children could use some help with the chores around here."

Kisemei listened quietly, his sobs subsiding.

"That is why you are here," she said, pacing back toward the boy as she leaned down toward his face once more. "Now—from today, you are my slave."

The last word cut into Kisemei with a jolt. *How could this be?* he wondered. *Oh, to just be back in the village on my own.* The loneliness of his short, brutal past was suddenly far more desirable than the prospect of slavery. *What will become of me? Why me?*

Over time, Kisemei would learn the answer to the last question. Kisemei, his father Kupe, and his stepmother had been living at a cattle ranch where Kupe was employed as a ranch hand. Several months earlier, while surveying the 5,000 bulls and seemingly innumerable cows that stretched out like a sea before him, Kupe had concocted a plan. Just as he had repeatedly done to his own stepfather, he would steal a cow from his new boss and sell it for a little extra money for himself. *There are so many heads of cattle,* Kupe thought. *They will never miss just one. And I need the money so very much.*

So with a plan in hand, Kupe waited for the perfect moment, grabbed the nose ring of a cow, and led it away to sell it, undetected. He then returned to the ranch to go about his daily chores as if nothing had happened.

But in the evening, a commotion arose among the cowboy and the ranchers.

"There is one missing. Count them again. Check their tags," the cowboy ordered.

Much to Kupe's horror, he discovered that at this ranch, every cow was numbered, and every evening there was a count of every cow. Soon there would be no question about what had happened. It was only a matter of deciphering who had done it. Kupe had been out herding the cattle that day, so the blame inevitably fell on him.

"Tell me where the missing cow is, Kupe," demanded the head cowboy. "What have you done with it?"

"I don't know!" exclaimed Kupe.

The number of free-range, wild beasts was slowly dwindling in the area, but it wasn't unheard of for a large cat or another predator to attack cattle in the area. "Maybe one of the lions got it," Kupe offered.

With that, the ranchers mounted their horses and rode off to investigate. As they rode, they noticed a trail of fresh hoofprints and footprints in the red dust that led away from the trampled field where the herd had grazed throughout the day. Following the trail, they ran across some men and asked them if they had seen the cow.

"Oh yes," said one of the men. "Kupe offered it to us for sale, and we bought it."

With that, Kupe's fate was sealed. The ranchers thundered back to the ranch on their horses and called to the hands nearby, pointing to Kupe. "Have this man arrested for theft!"

Kupe was bound and taken into the custody of the local police. As he was being led away, the foreman explained, "You will spend the night in jail. If you cannot produce the money to pay for the cow you sold, you will be taken to court, tried for theft, and sent to prison."

The next morning, Kupe sent a message to the ranch owner to meet him at the jail. A Maasai woman soon arrived at the jail to see Kupe. The widow of the former ranch owner, she was now the only proprietor of the ranch. Expecting immediate payment for her missing cow, she demanded to know where she could collect the money. Kupe explained, "I do not have the money for the cow yet because the men I sold it to arranged to purchase it under the condition that I would be paid once they had the opportunity to resell it. But please do not send me to prison," he begged.

The ranch owner was irate and promised that Kupe would stand trial that very day if he could not come up with payment. And with that, Kupe's cold heart thought of the one thing of significant value that he did have. Perhaps he could arrange a trade for his freedom after all.

"There is one thing I can offer you."

"And what is that?" paused the widow.

"My son."

"Your son?"

"Yes. He is very young, only about five years old. But he is strong and healthy, and with time he will grow into a very able-bodied man. Take him as your indentured servant in exchange for my freedom. Do with him as you please. He is yours. Just please do not send me to prison," begged Kupe, clutching the cold, paint-chipped bars of the jail cell.

The widow paused, pondering this offer for a minute. With the death of her husband, there was much manual labor left to be done around the ranch house. "I could use some help around the ranch. Okay. We have a deal. Tell me where I can find the boy, and I will send my men to get him right away. If we find the boy, I will not press charges. I will send word to you tomorrow whether or not we have found him. If we find him, I will call the police station, and they will let you go."

"Oh, thank you," Kupe celebrated. "Thank you, madam! He is at the home of my wife's cousin in the village. He is yours."

With this exchange, Kisemei's young life was destined for darker days. Innocent of any crime, he would spend the next several years working as a slave of the widow, paying the punishment for his father's sin. In his new role, he was provided with clothes and daily meals for the first time in quite a while. But even though he was of the age when most children entered primary school, he was deprived of any education. His time was to be devoted solely to serving the widow.

As soon as he arrived at the widow's ranch house, he was immediately put to work. The first task he was given was to carry 12 bottles of milk from the farm and deliver them over several miles to various houses in the area. It was a task that was too much for the small boy on his first day, and he found himself too weak for the heavy load. But even though he was but a small child, Kisemei was shown no mercy. When the farmers discovered that he had failed at his task, they beat him and threatened the same fate if he did not carry out the task as instructed the next day.

From that day forward, Kisemei delivered the milk, using a plan he had conceived in secret. He would carry all the bottles a short distance out of sight and then hide some of them under a bush while he delivered the rest. He would return for some other bottles and deliver them separately and keep returning to his stash until he had delivered everything. This added many additional miles of walking to his task every day, but it ensured that he would not be beaten.

It turned out that milk delivery was only his secondary daily task. Primarily he was charged with looking after the widow's milk calves. This was a task he was expected to do in every season and in all types of weather. Even during the rainy season, he stayed with the calves out in the field during the day, exposed to the elements. There were no vacations or holidays for Kisemei. Every day blended with the day before and the day after. The extraordinary task of indentured servitude became ordinary, relentless, and routine—every day, that is, except for one.

CHAPTER V

The Encounter

Although Kisemei's daily milk route was physically difficult for such a young child, there was one stop along the way that he enjoyed. The Nicklassons were a family of American missionaries who lived at the Africa Inland Mission in nearby Loitokitok. Although they were entirely unaware of Kisemei's predicament, they showed the boy kindness and friendship, always inviting him into their home when he came by with the daily milk delivery. It was a cherished reprieve from his otherwise grueling daily routine. He adjusted his delivery route so he would be sure to reach the missionaries' home last so he could stay there longer. Often they would give him treats such as lawa lawa sweets. In his early youth, Kisemei did not understand the message of Christianity they tried to share with him when he visited their home.

The endless routine of delivering milk during the morning and tending to the widow's calves during the afternoon and evening was the same every day, with days and weeks blurring into months and years, each day as ordinary as the next, until that one day.

It had begun like any other day that Kisemei lived recently. Two entire years had passed by then, and he was still faithfully performing the tasks the widow in the large, stone ranch house had given him.

One morning, walking the same road as he had on seemingly endless occasions for his morning milk deliveries, he passed a tall, slender Maasai man dressed in his crimson finest. Even though Kisemei was no more than seven years old, he remembered his Maasai roots. It was customary for a Maasai to stop on his way and greet another Maasai he may encounter.

So as the man approached, Kisemei stopped and greeted him with a traditional nod and said, "Gasak."

The Maasai man placed his hand on Kisemei's head and responded, "Eva, supa," or "Hello, young boy." Realizing the boy's youth and the time of day, he asked, "Why are you not in school?"

"I do not go to school," explained Kisemei.

"Where do you live?" asked the man. "Where is your family?"

Kisemei explained all that had transpired. He told him his name, who his parents were, the village from which he came, the fate that had befallen him when his father was arrested for stealing a cow, and how his father had sold him into slavery.

As the man listened, his smile melted to a grim, sad gaze that suddenly rose to a glare of urgency. "Kisemei, you and I are family!" he exclaimed. "Your father and I are distant cousins." With a helpless gasp of surprise, Kisemei looked up at the man and began to smile. "You can help me?"

The man pondered this predicament for a while. Kisemei anxiously studied the man's face, watching as he glanced from place to place as he thought. In a moment, the product of his contemplation was complete. Kneeling down and resting his hand on Kisemei's shoulder, he concluded, "I must help you. I will do what I can. Do not tell anyone else that we have spoken. Go on your way, and I will find you."

"Thank you, sir. Thank you." Kisemei smiled as he picked up the milk bottles with a newfound wave of energy.

"You are welcome, cousin," the man called out. Looking back with a start that thrust a puff of dust loose from the road, the man added, "Remember, do not tell anyone we have spoken."

"Oh, yes, I will remember. Thank you," came the small boy's muffled, distant response.

The man and Kisemei both went on their separate routes, both with hastened strides. Kisemei's cousin set about on a 30-mile route directly to his home to tell his mother the news about the young cousin he had just met. The news quickly reached Kisemei's uncles. The next day, one of the uncles went to tell the local government officials that he knew of a boy who was not attending school.

Many days had passed since Kisemei had met his cousin on the road. It seemed like it had been an eternity, and still, nothing had changed. Kisemei was bursting with an anxious desire to tell someone about his unusual encounter, but just as he had promised, he kept the visit a secret, carrying on with his chores as usual.

One afternoon while he was hard at work in the fields near the widow's large, stone house, the sound of approaching cars began to rise in the distance. Vehicles were not an uncommon sight at the widow's farm, but on this occasion, several vehicles were approaching at once and at a rapid pace. It was a pace Kisemei had seen on a similar road once before. The sight was unsettling at first, reminding him of the series of events that occurred the day he was kidnapped by the two men in the Land Rover. But it also rekindled that battered, frail glimmer of hope that maybe, just maybe, someone was finally coming for him to take him away from his life of bondage. Hearing the commotion near the house, Kisemei led the cattle he was tending in a direction where he could see what was happening. Near the house were two police cars and several men in Kenyan police uniforms. But there were three other people with them. One of them looked very familiar. Wincing as he craned his neck, a jolt of joy overtook him as he realized who it was.

It is my mother! And my uncle! Kisemei's soul cried out inside of him. A rush of courage pressed him closer. *And my father's cousin, the one I met on the road. They have come for me!* He would soon learn that the other person was one of his uncles.

Kisemei could hear the muffled voices of the widow and the police officers echoing through the windows of the large, stone farmhouse. What they were saying was unintelligible, but they were discernibly engaged in a stern if not heated conversation. The solid soles of the uniformed officers' boots could be heard clumping and shifting on the wooden floor as they methodically worked their way through the house. As Kisemei's hope continued to rise, it fostered the courage to approach the house. The stern, muffled voices grew louder until the back door groaned open, releasing the end of the conversation to the warm, Kenyan air. ". . . will be taking the boy with us, and that is final. You there! What is your name, son?"

"Kisemei, sir." The policemen methodically advanced toward him while Kisemei stood in cautious repose.

Before memories could record another moment, Kisemei found himself in the careful grasp of the officers who escorted him past the bewildered gaze of the widow and her children and deposited him in the back seat of a police car beside his long-lost mother, Leah. The door shut, the engines started, and the cars carried the group beyond the sight of the far gate of the ranch. Hasty embraces and sobbing greetings and exchanges pent up from years of absence let loose between mother and son.

After Kisemei's father's cousin and uncle had contacted the local government and told their friends and family what they had discovered, the news of Kisemei's whereabouts spread throughout his former community. The local government then contacted the local police who made plans to rescue the boy.

According to Kenyan law, all children of Kisemei's age were required to attend school. Although the Maasai were usually left to live and govern by their own laws, schooling for all children from first grade through middle school was compulsory, regardless of tribal affiliation. Ironically, it was upon those grounds that the government was moved to act and not necessarily as a result of the boy's indentured servitude, even though such forms of slavery were not allowed in the Maasai tribe.

Kisemei was finally free, but fear of his recapture lingered not only in the young boy's wounded heart but also in the minds of those members of his family who now had custody of him. It was still possible that he could be kidnapped again and gone without a trace. In order to ensure his safety, officials sent Kisemei away to a government-operated district education boarding school in Loitokitok, Kenya, a type of rescue center designed to help Maasai children.

There Kisemei began to thrive. It was the first formal education he had encountered. And it was also the first time in his life that he was able to just be a child without the pressures of survival. But it was not to last.

As the holiday season approached and the first semester drew to a close, it was time for Kisemei to go home to his family until the start of the new semester. The students began leaving one by one as their parents arrived to take them home. Kisemei waited anxiously, regularly glancing out the windows as far down the road as his gaze could reach in the direction he expected someone would arrive.

As the number of students dwindled to just a few, one of the teachers became concerned. "Who is coming to get you?" he asked.

"My father," Kisemei admitted with a tone of dismay.

But he did not see his father. As time passed to the end of the day, Kisemei was the last student remaining on the campus. Inevitably, a day passed into several, and it became painfully clear that Kisemei's father was not coming for him. He could not live on his own on a closed campus. In a way, he was like an orphan yet again. It was with a grateful heart that Kisemei soon learned that several of the teachers had decided to take turns letting him stay with them until the end of the semester break.

It was customary in Maasai culture that if a full dowry was paid to his family, as had been done by Leah's family many years prior, their children remained in the father's custody no matter what circumstances may unfold. Therefore, it was expected that Kisemei would continue to live with Kupe, despite the bleak prospects his father afforded him through neglect and destitution.

At the start of the new semester, however, the government's Department of Education contacted Kisemei's parents. His father, Kupe, remained destitute, and it was clear he had been negligent in the care of his son. Leah, Kisemei's biological mother, was able to demonstrate that although she led a meager life, she could provide for Kisemei financially, especially compared to his father. And if times became rough again, she also had the support of her brothers. Therefore, the authorities forced Kupe to sign papers that officially granted full custody of Kisemei to Leah. So Kisemei left the boarding school and returned to live with his mother for the first time since his parents had divorced. But without a husband to provide support, Leah constantly faced the pangs of poverty. She struggled to support Kisemei and her other children, raising what money she could by selling onions in the rural market.

Even in these moments of hardship, Kisemei's mother taught her children humility and respect for others, and she taught them to participate in the hard work of the household. Kisemei's siblings shared the chores, but as the oldest, he had the most responsibilities. They included cleaning the house, collecting water and firewood, preparing food, washing dishes, and helping cultivate the family garden.

This existence proved too meager to provide enough extra money to send Kisemei back to the boarding school. After only one semester of classes, Kisemei once again found himself without an education. It would be another two years before he set foot in a classroom again.

At the age of 10 or 11, with only half a year of first-grade education to his name, Kisemei was finally able to enroll in Kimana Primary School. It was a small school located just up the road from his mother's home. There was only enough food for Kisemei to eat one meal a day. Rarely able to have breakfast or lunch, he found it hard to concentrate on an empty stomach. He wore the same tattered uniform every day and always walked to school barefoot. Even so, Kisemei proved to be an average student with a great passion for books. Although he found his classes difficult, he was grateful and persisted through the hardships. He later recalled, "It was only by the grace of God that I got to read and write."

CHAPTER VI

Something More

Now growing tall and slender like the other young Maasai men, Kisemei was about 13 years old when his uncles approached him with the news. "It is now time for you to become a Moran."

A Moran was a young Maasai warrior. It was considered a great honor to become a young warrior among the Maasai, and it was a rite of passage steeped in ritual and mysticism. It would be a long, relatively expensive, and daunting task that Kisemei, his family, and his village held sacred. Once a Moran, there would be no going back.

A protracted sequence of ceremonial events commenced that would both symbolically and physically guide Kisemei's metamorphosis into a Moran and by this process pass into manhood.

The first ceremony was called Enkipaata. During this event, Kisemei and the other young trainees of his generation were led out into the grassy wilderness of the Kenyan plains. Over about four months, the boys, led by a group of local elders, gained instruction in the ways of the Maa culture. After this process, the boys were ceremonially unwrapped, symbolizing their impending transformation into a new age of early manhood.

Kisemei's family then celebrated Orkiteng le Ntomono, a ceremony intended just for him when a bull from his family's herd was slaughtered. In the subsequent family ceremony of Olker lo Kitupukinet, a lamb was slaughtered. There was also the ceremony of Enkitoto, which was conducted in preparation for circumcision.

After a significant period, it was time for Eunoto o Latimi. Like the other boys in the ceremony, Kisemei's head was shaved, and he was led into the forest to find a long pole that he brought back to his mother's house to be placed nearby. Every day of the ceremony, women danced around this pole while the young warriors entertained the Laibon, one of the senior elders of the village and also the healer and spiritual guide. The boys would stay with this community for one year before joining the ranks of the Moran.

Then it was time for Emurata, one of the most important ceremonies in the Maasai culture. This ceremony was the main rite of passage intended for the village's youth of both genders. For girls, the ceremonial process was comparatively simple. But for boys such as Kisemei, a series of strenuous tasks were required to be completed without complaint in order to prove to the clan that they were ready to become men. They involved activities such as carrying heavy weaponry and herding many cattle at a time.

Kisemei and the other boys were led out to herd cattle for seven straight days, remaining out in the elements for the duration. In the early morning on the day of the conclusion of the ceremony, the boys were doused with cold water while friends and family looked on, shouting words of encouragement and occasionally insults as the youths stood perfectly still and silent. This was intentionally performed during a season when cold air had descended on the village. Should they manage to tolerate the ordeal without the slightest protest, they would be considered successful. Should they relinquish even the slightest flinch, they would be considered outcasts. Subsequently for about four to six months, the boys were dressed in black as a symbol of this time of transition.

Boys who completed the final stages of the process were considered full-fledged Moran—young warriors. Likewise, girls who completed their journey through Emurata were considered adults and were allowed to marry.

Kisemei stood strong through it all and became a Moran. He donned the iconic ornate, crimson Moran attire and bore the same manner of weaponry as countless generations of his tribe since times long before recorded history began. And perhaps most pivotal of all, he took an oath of allegiance to the ways and rituals of the Maasai, forsaking all other traditions and philosophies, vowing to shun all religions and any other culture but his own.

And so it was that Kisemei completed the ceremonies, took the oath, and stood among the ranks of his forefathers as a faithful member of the world-famous Maasai warriors. As a Moran, he was considered among those of the tribe to be complete—a young adult, a young man fit to serve and defend the ancient order of the Maasai.

With the title of Moran came also a new heightened level of responsibility. Although he had struggled in school in the past, he had always done his best when given the opportunity to learn. But now as a Moran, he was expected to be excellent.

The gauntlet of training and ceremonies was finally behind him, and Kisemei knew that he had achieved a status that garnered great honor among his tribe and, indeed, his nation. He was willing to accept the higher personal expectations that came with Moranism, and he took pride in the title he had earned.

But to Kisemei, it was a time of emptiness. He felt as though his new life was lacking in some intangible, indescribable manner. The pressures of his title and the lack of fulfillment it produced continued to erode at Kisemei until finally he decided there simply must be something missing in his life that he had not yet found.

It was a feeling that compelled him to search for answers. In middle school, he encountered students from other African cultures who spoke of a being that encompassed and controlled all that is around us, an entity some called God. Others spoke of a similar being they called Allah. He was curious what this being might be, but through his background, he knew of nothing but Maasai culture that spoke of no such being.

At school, his curiosity led him to visit a classmate who regularly attended a local mosque. "I want to learn more about God. Can you tell me what you know?" he asked.

"Come with me to the mosque on Friday," invited his classmate. "I will introduce you to someone who can tell you more."

That week, Kisemei and his friend went to the mosque where Kisemei was introduced to an Islamic missionary. The missionary invited him to join the local soccer team sponsored by the mosque. The Muslim missionaries formed these soccer teams as a way to reach the local Kenyan youth.

"But I have no money for uniforms or equipment," said Kisemei.

The missionary patted Kisemei on the back. "It is okay. We will give you a new uniform and new shoes. Come and join us."

For the next three months, Kisemei regularly attended the mosque with his classmate and played soccer with their team. It wasn't long before the sheikh invited him to convert to Islam.

At that time, Muslim missionaries in that part of Africa mainly focused their efforts on the tribes in Tanzania who were more receptive to their message. They had historically found the Maasai to be hostile toward Islam. The prospect of a Maasai Moran converting to Islam was quite unusual, an opportunity in which his Muslim friends were quite interested.

By then, Kisemei was deeply immersed in the traditions of the Maasai. After all, he had taken an oath as a Moran and was now steeped in the height of the Maasai culture. Dying his hair the traditional red and clad in the traditional crimson garb of a young warrior, his primary allegiance remained loyally devoted to the covenants he had made with his tribe.

Yet, even so, Kisemei did not have to ponder the sheikh's invitation for long. He saw no reason not to convert to Islam, as long as his family approved.

When he arrived home, he could hardly wait to tell his mother the news. "I must tell you all about Allah," he explained.

"Allah?" his mother cautiously asked.

"Yes, Mother. I want to become a Muslim and study more about Allah, but first I need your permission."

"Kisemei," she said, "I do not know anything about this Allah or this Islam about which you speak, but it is okay with me if you want to learn more about it, only if it does not interfere with the Maasai culture and your duties as a Moran."

"I assure you, Mother, it will not."

"Then it is okay."

And with those words, Kisemei fervently began his Islamic studies. He devoted a significant amount of his free time to reading the Quran between middle school classes, and he began to adopt the daily ritual of Islamic prayers facing Mecca and weekly trips to the mosque. It is common for a new Islamic convert for his Islamic teachers to change his name as a way to symbolize his newfound devotion to this religion. They began to call him "Yahayah," which is Arabic for Isaiah.

As Kisemei's transformation progressed, unsettling darkness began to rest on him as he lay down to sleep at night. Soon he would meet the architect of his nightmares face to face.

CHAPTER VII

The Awakening

Kisemei's days were long and busy with his time divided between middle school classes, prayer, religious studies, adherence to Maasai traditions, and helping his mother. Such active daily life had always left Kisemei quite capable of a deep, rejuvenating sleep in the past, but lately, circumstances had changed.

It had begun suddenly one night and persisted every night thereafter. He found himself dreading the inevitable slumber that awaited him. His friends began to notice that he was groggy and distant during the day. Clearly, something was wrong, and they wanted to know what it was.

Kisemei did his best to explain. "I have this dream. It comes to me every night now. It frightens me so. I wake up shaking and covered in sweat. I cannot make it stop. Every night it comes to me."

Concerned, one of his friends asked, "What happens in this dream?"

Kisemei pondered quietly for a moment, and then gazing off into the distance, he began. "I find myself falling into the center of a very deep pit with fire burning far below me. I land on a small rock in the center of the pit. There I stand up, but I cannot raise my hands. The rock shifts beneath my feet, and I have to struggle to keep my balance as the flames lash up around me. It is so hot! I am so afraid! I look up, and the edge of the pit is so far away."

Breathing heavily, Kisemei paused to regain his composure and then continued. "I see a bright light beyond the opening. I call out, 'Jesus, help me,' and a bright, white hand rushes into the pit, grabs me, and pulls me out."

"Jesus?" one friend interrupted.

"Let him finish," scolded another.

Kisemei looked up at them and then away again. "The heat subsides, and I find myself surrounded by a brilliant, white light. It is so glorious, so comforting." Then slowly smiling, he added, "And then through the blaze of light I can begin to see a figure—a man, shining white as brightly as the sun—reaching out to me. I can clearly see the open wounds on his hands and his feet as he approaches. He has such a beautiful smile. And he calls to me, 'Come and follow me.'"

His friends looked on with subdued yet troubled expressions as he spoke. Eventually, one responded. "This Jesus is Jeshua, the prophet spoken of in the Quran. He is only a prophet, Kisemei."

During his Islamic training, Kisemei had been taught that Jesus was merely a prophet and that Christians were not actually members of a legitimate religious organization since the Quran teaches that Allah never gave birth to a son.

Another friend, a Muslim woman, offered her insight. "You are being visited by a genie—a ghost. Female genies wear black and are a bad omen, but male genies wear white and are considered a blessing. So, congratulations! Consider yourself blessed. Now try to find a way to get some sleep, and do not worry about these dreams any longer."

Kisemei did try to put the dream out of his mind and go about his daily life as usual, even though the dream persisted intrusively each night as he slept.

During that time, he often spent time in his village tending to his mother's farm. It was around noon one hot summer Saturday while Kisemei and his sisters were resting from their chores around the farm that he noticed four Tanzanian men walking through the village. Kisemei had just finished cleaning up and was brushing his red-painted hair when he noticed that all the men were carrying books.

Those are Bibles, he thought. As he watched them, he noticed they were methodically stopping and visiting the people of his village, going from house to house. *That means they will come here. I cannot let them bother me!*

Instinctively, he rushed into the one-room house to avoid detection. The village hut had no locking door, so he knew an encounter was inevitable. He resolved *to hide until they leave.*

Glancing beside him, he noticed the straw bed and leaped into it, tossing a blanket over him and falling motionless in an instant. *I will pretend to be asleep so they cannot trouble me,* he thought as he waited for the men to pass by.

As he lay there on the bed alone on that hot Kenyan afternoon, Kisemei began to perceive the thatched roof of the house lifting clear of its earthen bracing. Suddenly, though shrouded in the darkness of his blanket, he found himself consumed with the sensation of being engulfed in a brilliant, white, shining light. It felt hot as though it were blazing straight against his face and chest even though he was still covered by the blanket. His heart began to race as he found himself consumed with fear. Terror gripped his eyes shut as though it was before a moment of a great impact, and he was unable to open them despite his best immediate efforts.

As his terror heightened, he heard a voice right next to him ask," Why are you running? Why are you running from me?"

Now, completely consumed with fear, his pulse pounded at the wall of his chest to the point that it felt like it would surely break through. Finally, Kisemei was able to open his eyes and look around. There was no one in the room but him. The bright light was gone. The roof of the house was intact. Kisemei sat up, now drenched in sweat and greatly fatigued from the experience.

In a moment, he heard a stranger greeting him at the doorway.

"Hello. May I come in?"

"Yes," relented Kisemei.

Slowly walking into the house, the man dragged a chair from across the room to the bed where Kisemei was still sitting.

"My name is Paul," introduced the stranger. "I love Jesus. He is my Lord and Savior, and we are here to share the love of Christ with you."

There was nothing left to be said. Kisemei had been through many experiences that had led up to this moment, including the one that had just occurred only minutes beforehand. Kisemei was sure how he would respond. He looked up, and with his eyes locked with the visitors, he replied, "My name is Kisemei, and I am not a Christian. But today I want to be one."

With those words came a rush of relief from deep within his heart. It was instantly overwhelming. Kisemei burst into tears.

CHAPTER VIII

A New Beginning

Paul motioned for them to kneel together. There in the dusty, red-dirt-floor, single-room, mud-and-dung house, they prayed together for over 30 minutes. They prayed for repentance. They prayed for guidance. And finally, Kisemei prayed for Jesus to save him and take control of his life.

At the utterance of the last amen of this prayer, Kisemei was filled with an intense, overwhelming, rejuvenating sense of joy. It was as though an unbearable burden was instantly lifted from his shoulders. It was a feeling he had never experienced before in his life.

"I feel such joy! Such joy and peace!" he told Paul. "It is a joy that is not found anywhere in my culture. I want to tell everyone what I feel!"

The two men then conversed together for a while with laughter and an emboldened exchange of celebration and gratitude. Before long, it was time for Paul to be on his way. He gave Kisemei a Bible, invited him to attend church the following Sunday, and left to continue on through the village.

Everything was new. Even though Kisemei was surrounded by the same family and tribe, even though he remained committed to the ways of the Maasai warriors, and even though the sun still rose above Kilimanjaro just as before, it was as if everything had been reset, rejuvenated, and refreshed. But it was an experience that had not been shared by the others in his village.

To Kisemei, his experience had been genuine, so profound that he found himself continuing to burst with the desire to tell others what had happened. He went to find his mother. She had supported him when he decided to study Islam, so surely she would be supportive of this new experience as well. After all, he remained committed to his oaths as a Moran.

Kisemei told his mother everything that had happened. He explained that he was going to start attending a Christian church. Her response was not what he had expected.

"I do not want you to go to a Christian church," she quickly replied.

"But Mother, I must go! The missionary explained how important it was that I . . ."

His mother interrupted. "I said no, Kisemei." She turned and looked firmly into his eyes with the countenance of solemn worry. "No. You must not." Looking away, she explained, "I am afraid . . ."

"Afraid of what, Mother?" he consoled.

"I am afraid for you now, Kisemei—afraid for your future, afraid you will abandon your culture and your people. You are a Maasai—and not just a Maasai, you are a Moran, my son. I was not worried when you wanted to study Islam because those who do, don't change. They remain as they were. But those who convert to following Jesus abandon their culture. They change completely. You must not abandon the ways of the Maasai. I do not give you permission to do this!"

Kisemei reassured his mother that this would not happen. "I have sworn an oath to my people and to my fellow Moran. I am a Maasai warrior, and I will always be so. I am still a Moran. I am still your son, Mother."

It was all so new to him, this commitment to Jesus. The encounters he had experienced reassured him of the validity of his new path. The metamorphosis in the pit of his being drove him onward with a testimony of sincerity, but it was all brand new to him. In a way, for a short time he found himself alone, orphan-like again, like a new-sprung bloom in a desert of souls, unguided, unnurtured, and all together unaware of what peril awaited him in the path of this new journey he had chosen.

Just as his mother said, Kisemei had also observed many times that the Muslims he encountered remained entirely unchanged after their conversions to their faith. His Islamic peers would undertake ritualistic cleansing and praying before and during their trip to the mosque but would return to their regular ways for the rest of the week, living just as they had before they met the Muslim missionaries. The idea that any other faith would compel someone to live entirely set apart from their old ways after a conversion experience was entirely unknown to him at that time.

At first, life continued as before for Kisemei. Before his encounter with the Christian missionary, he and his friends had already set in motion a plan to join a local gang. So that afternoon, Kisemei went about the prearranged plan to earn the money necessary to pay his way into the gang's initiation process by collecting sand to load onto trucks for cash. By evening, enough money was collected, and the boys paid their initiation fees to the gang leader.

News was prone to spread quickly in the village. By this time, the gang leader had heard of Kisemei's testimony of his Christian conversion.

"What are you boys doing tonight?" he asked.

"Nothing really," the boys replied.

"Come to my house," invited the man. "Let's have a party to celebrate—to welcome you all into the gang. It will be fun!"

The man was known among the villagers as someone who seemed to have a degree of natural wisdom about life, and he was often eager to share his insights. But that day was different. He did not believe the stories that Kisemei told of his recent conversion, and he was determined to prove they were false by testing him and his friends.

That night, Kisemei and his friends set out for the house where the party was to be held.

As Kisemei was walking, he heard a loud voice calling out to him from beside the road. "Kisemei! Kisemei! Where are you going?"

Turning to see who it was, he saw a woman standing nearby in the direction of the voice, so he approached her. "Did you say something to me?"

"No, sir, I did not call to you," she replied.

"My apologies," nodded Kisemei, and he continued on with his friends.

"Kisemei! Kisemei! Where are you going?" called the stranger's voice again just as clearly and close by as before. Kisemei stopped and looked around, but this time there was no one nearby but his friends.

"What's wrong?" one of his friends asked. "Did you hear someone again?"

"No, it must be nothing," he concluded, and they continued walking.

But the same voice called out to him a third time, just as close as before. "Kisemei! Kisemei! Where are you going?"

Even so, Kisemei was determined to carry on. After all, he saw no one speaking to him. It was just a party like any other, and he was with his friends. *What could be the harm in that?* he reasoned.

As they approached the house, the commotion of laughter and music escaped through the windows with the sound of a boiling pot in the background. As they reached the doorway, a thick, white, pungent mist of opium smoke rolled out into the evening air, revealing glimpses of all manner of illicit activities waiting inside. The other boys gladly continued through the door past the nude figures, through the smoke, and around the bongs on the floor to take their places among the other guests. But Kisemei hesitated at the door.

The man who invited them saw Kisemei standing at the door. "Ah, you have made it. We have been waiting for you. Come in." The man put up his arms and gestured welcomingly. "Come in! God is here," he laughed as his guests joined in with chuckles and taunts.

Kisemei felt a bolt of anger rush to his head. The words burst through his lips as quickly as they had arrived. "Don't you know that I am born again and Jesus is my Lord and Savior . . ."

"How dare you mention that name before me!" interrupted the man.

"Yes! It is true! I was saved this morning," volleyed Kisemei as he thrust his finger toward the host of the party. "Look what you are doing! You are going to perish with your sins. And I am *not* going to do what you are doing." And with that, Kisemei spun around and left.

CHAPTER IX

The Challenge

The next morning was Sunday. Despite the urging of his mother and the taunting of his peers, Kisemei set out for the church in the nearby town.

Although he had regularly worshiped at a mosque for the past two years, this new experience at a Christian worship service was unlike anything he had encountered before. He was quite accustomed to long sermons by the Islamic leaders that were cast out over the attendees of the mosque mixed with recitations from the Quran. But at the Christian church, a woman preacher spoke from the Bible. Even though the sanctuary was full of worshippers, the verses she quoted from Isaiah 38 seemed to be spoken right to him alone. It felt as if she were pointing these words right at him: "Put your house in order, because you are going to die; you will not recover."

Through the course of the sermon, Kisemei became convinced he had received a message from God.

I have only a short time to prepare my house before I'm going to die, he thought. *I want to turn away from my old ways. Yesterday God told me to go to church and stay away from that party. I should have known not to go to that house.*

At the end of the service, Kisemei went to the front of the church, and the congregation prayed for him. It was there that Kisemei fully committed to turning away from the ways of his past and living every day for his new Savior, Jesus.

The next day was a regular school day, and Kisemei returned to middle school classes as usual. His mentor was quite fond of him. She was a Muslim woman who was a Swahili teacher.

"Good morning, Kisemei. How was your weekend?" she asked.

"Good morning, ma'am. Oh, it was wonderful," he replied.

"You are doing well in school. Soon you will complete your middle school training and will be ready for high school classes. The sheikh is impressed with you too. You are the first Maasai to convert to Islam, you know." She smiled at him with pride. "He is planning to send you to Saudi Arabia this summer for Islamic training."

Hesitantly, Kisemei responded, "I have changed my mind. You see, I am a Christian now."

The teacher sat up straight with surprise. "A Christian?" she repeated. "What on earth makes you think you are a Christian now?"

Kisemei told her all that had happened and the way his life had changed. But his mentor was not impressed. Instead, she grew very concerned. Later that day, she told the sheikh leaders about this latest development.

Soon, the sheikh leaders and Kisemei's teacher returned to speak with Kisemei, books in hand. But this time they were not carrying copies of the Quran. They were carrying Bibles.

"You have been misinformed, Kisemei," they said. "Here. Let us show you in the Christian Scriptures how the Christian teachings are wrong."

"They are telling you things that are contrary to the Quran," another said. "They are liars!"

At that moment, a rush came over Kisemei. He could feel himself becoming filled with a forceful, uncontrollable drive to speak. In Arabic, he interrupted the sheikh leaders as his teacher looked on.

"You do not know the power of the one true living God. If you did, you would not speak this way. You teach these things, but you have never met God. I have, and I have repented from my old ways. You must repent, too, or you will perish."

Those present with Kisemei were astonished at the words he spoke. With zealous passion, Kisemei began to speak to them about the saving power of Jesus, and he continued to urge them all to repent. He spoke with authority and confidence his friends were unaccustomed to. It was more than they could bear. They had nothing further to say.

"Instead," he later recalled, "they all just got up and ran away."

Kisemei's teacher absorbed this whole experience. She was no longer concerned for Kisemei. Instead, she began to become concerned about her own direction in life. It was through this event that she, too, left Islam and committed her life to Christ.

CHAPTER X

Strengthening Ties, Loosening Ties

The Maasai are a pastoral people who have lived a life deeply immersed in tradition and family since time immemorial. The covenants they make with one another are for a lifetime. While most of the other African tribes have abandoned their ancient traditions, the Maasai have resisted change. Roaming the African plain, they once followed the rain, raising nomadic herds of cattle, sheep, and goats, not to eat but rather as a kind of currency, measuring their wealth by the size of their herds. Though now they are confined to the boundaries of the lands set aside for them, livestock, tradition, and family remain inseparable in the fabric of the Maasai culture.

The phenomenon perpetuating this cultural preservation has been partially precipitated by international curiosity. From diets mostly consisting of meat, milk, and blood to the innumerable ceremonies throughout the Maasai calendar, to the spectacular adornments and proximity to various natural wonders and wildlife preserves, there is much to experience in a Maasai village. From naming a baby to circumcision, to childhood, to Moran, to young adults, to junior elders, and finally to elders, the arrival of each new stage of life is marked by elaborate ceremonies for every Maasai. Tall and slender, Maasai warriors with their long, red-dyed hair have become a photogenic icon of the Kenyan national identity. Tourists travel on safaris to visit their villages and experience this increasingly rare ancient way of life.

For other ancient cultures in the modern world, the lure of change is ubiquitous, relentless, and, in some circumstances, an increasingly practical option for some Maasai villagers. Driven in part by perpetually receding grazing lands, some are taking jobs in towns and cities and living in houses as a way to survive. Lands that for innumerable generations were the immeasurably vast, eternal hunting grounds of the Maasai people are now government-controlled wildlife sanctuaries and national parks, and beyond those boundaries are ranches, towns, and cities.

The forces of change that we find in the Maasai today were also present in the time of Kisemei's youth. Although these changes were external, permanent change had already taken root in Kisemei's spiritual life. Nevertheless, keenly aware of the creeping secular socioeconomic changes around him, it was with a deep sense of duty and honor that Kisemei was determined to remain committed to his tribal oaths and loyally adhere to the ways of the Maasai warriors, even with the newfound light of Jesus in his heart. At first, this seemed like the only possible solution.

From the dramatic encounters Kisemei had experienced, he knew without a shadow of a doubt that the power of his salvation was real and binding and that he would remain forever loyal to his Savior whom he loved. But Kisemei also loved his family and his heritage. Despite the many hardships and dark moments, he was proud of his status as a Maasai warrior and remained committed to honoring his family and his cultural traditions. But soon he began to realize that the practices and beliefs of the Maasai warriors were in many ways contradictory to the teachings of the Christian faith. One could not coexist with the other in their life. They were mutually exclusive. To truly live committed to one would mean to forsake the other. That revelation began to torment Kisemei. He knew he would never leave Jesus who against such great odds and under such extraordinary circumstances had relentlessly pursued him and had never left him or forsaken him. But he also did not want to hurt his family. To denounce his culture would be devastating to them. And to abandon the Maasai warrior culture was unacceptable among his tribesmen.

It would be painful. It could even mean a death sentence. Yet Kisemei knew there was no other way. He knew what he must do.

According to Maasai tradition, a Moran was not permitted to eat alone or eat fatty meat in the house. When a Maasai warrior slaughtered an animal to eat, they were to go to the bushlands near the village and share the meat with the other warriors. This rule was set in place to ensure that all the warriors would be fed regardless of their economic status and also to ensure that the food they were eating was separate from the provisions available for their families. Kisemei knew that if he broke this rule, the action would be more fruitful than simply telling his family that he was leaving the ranks of the Maasai warriors. It would be a binding breech of Maasai law that would ensure he would be irrevocably ostracized from his warrior brethren. Afterward, the only question that would remain was just how severe those binding consequences would be.

As he took the meat into his mother's house alone in full view of the villagers, the gravity of that moment weighed heavily on Kisemei with physical intensity. Fear took hold of him, restraining his limbs like a vice as he forced onward with his plan. His body and hands trembled as he held the meat in front of him, ready to eat. Whatever the consequences, there was no turning back once he began to eat. Would they beat him? Would they banish him? Would they kill him? Because of the sermon he heard at church only weeks before, he was convinced that his fate was the latter. Even so, Kisemei knew that he must press on. He would not forsake Jesus, not even if it meant death. And so he began to eat the fatty meat alone in the house yet somehow remarkably visible to the curious, prying eyes of the astonished villagers.

Just as Kisemei had predicted, the news of this egregious breach of warrior protocol began to spread rapidly throughout the Maasai village. The essence of the news was not necessarily the specifics of how Kisemei had eaten alone but instead that he had abandoned Moranism and the Maasai culture, just as he had expected they would say. Over time, which seemed mere moments, everything was different.

When Kisemei's grandmother found out what had happened, she was incensed and confronted Kisemei with the accusations. "Is it true? Is it true what they say you have done? Have you disobeyed me? Have you broken your promise to your family and to your Maasai brethren? Answer me!"

"Yes, Grandmother, it is true."

Before he could begin to explain further, his grandmother, filled with rage, ran at him, chasing him from her house and yelling, "From today you are not part of this family!" Her words echoed off the adobe huts of the village as the people looked on.

My whole world has turned against me, Kisemei thought to himself as he ran for the relative safety of the nearby bushlands.

As time passed, Kisemei mustered the courage to approach his grandmother's house. He would seek refuge there in exchange for helping tend to her cattle. Although she agreed, the respite was short-lived. Within a matter of days, everything would change.

CHAPTER XI

The Valley of the Shadow of Death

Early one morning as the still, gentle glow of sunlight began to rise across the valley, Kisemei was startled awake by a cry of distress outside his grandmother's house.

"My grandson! Today he is going to die!"

Kisemei leapt from his cot. Peeking through the corner of the small, unglazed window in the rough clay-and-cow-dung wall, he could see assembled outside the house a large party of Maasai warriors in full regalia, about 150 in all, arranged shoulder to shoulder and circling the house with weapons in hand.

The men have come, he thought to himself. *They expect me to repent and leave Christianity.*

A provision existed in the Maasai law to allow a wayward warrior to reenter the ranks of his brothers if he would take a large bull owned by his family and slaughter it. After removing the bull's large intestine, a hole would be cut at each end of the bull, and the offending warrior would be pushed through the length of the bull's carcass, only to be washed in milk as he emerged from the posterior of the animal. Thus, he could be ceremonially baptized as a symbol of the abandonment of his past grievances, his renouncement of Christianity, and the affirmation of his recommitment to his life as a Moran. Kisemei knew that with the assemblage of such a force of warriors if he did not agree to participate in this ceremony, he would certainly be killed. He knew that under such circumstances, it was customary for the warriors to demolish an offending family member's home, bury them alive in the rubble, and leave them to die. Of this fate, Kisemei was now certain. They would not deviate from this tradition once the elders set it into motion. A Maasai would not dare question or contradict an elder's authority. Once the leader of the warriors decided to assemble the others to come for Kisemei, It was expected that each warrior would participate in the command to kill Kisemei without question or hesitation.

For a moment, Kisemei lay back on the cot to gather his thoughts. He knew he would not abandon Jesus. He loved Jesus no matter the consequences, and he was prepared for death. Even so, he did not want the warriors to destroy his grandmother's home. She had built it with her own hands, and she was not at fault for Kisemei's actions.

I will go outside and face them, he resolved. *I am ready to die.*

With a slow sigh, he closed his eyes and began to pray.

"God, if my enemy faces me in one way, will you despise them and send them away in seven ways? God, if you are real, do this today. But if you are ready to send me to heaven today, I am going to die."

And so he opened his eyes, stood up from his cot, pulled back the curtain from the doorway, and went outside.

As Kisemei emerged from the house, his grandmother, who had been anxiously awaiting the warriors' next move, ran for cover.

Time seemed to stand still as Kisemei was left to face the warriors alone. He stepped through the doorway of this grandmother's house and went into the still, cool air of the morning sun. He straightened bravely and looked straight ahead into the eyes of the encircling warriors. They stared back at him in still, silent anticipation as Kisemei stood motionless, awaiting his fate.

The warriors were taken aback by Kisemei's actions. He simply walked out and faced them. He had not attempted to fight or defend himself.

Suddenly, the leader of the group of warriors broke his stern composure, turned, and looked around to speak to the rest of them, "No, we are not going to beat this man. Who is it among you that goes to school? No one." Turning and pointing at Kisemei, he continued. "But this man, he goes to school. He is better than us. He knows a lot more than us. This man—he must have something we do not see."

The Maasai rules did not allow anyone to argue with a figure of authority, especially a warrior. Nevertheless, the other warriors were astonished at these words, and one of them could not resist the urge to respond. "No! He must be punished." That resulted in short order with the leader briskly clubbing the dissenter across the head. The dissenter began to bleed from the attack, and like a toppling of dominos, a complete collapse of command thus erupted among them all. The circle of warriors quickly collapsed into clusters of scuffling, arguing men and boys tossing, punching, and clubbing each other, and eventually scattering and parting ways in different directions without once turning to engage Kisemei.

All the while, Kisemei had remained motionless and silent as he stood in front of his grandmother's home. As quickly as it had begun, it had ended. Kisemei continued to stand and watch, entirely unscathed and untouched. As he watched the fighting clusters of warriors subside and walk away, he took a mental note to count the number of directions their trails of footsteps had left as they went. "One, two, three, four . . ."

"They have left in seven directions!" he realized. "They have literally despised each other and have been scattered in seven ways." Such an event was unprecedented in the verbal history of the Maasai, but it was unfolding all around Kisemei. He and his family realized that within the bounds of Maasai law, no further tribal reprimand would come. No one would attempt to harm him again. It was a humbling answer to his prayer for which he would remain eternally grateful.

CHAPTER XII

A New Direction

Although Kisemei's physical safety was secure, the consequences of a relationship with Jesus in his culture remained severe. Every member of his family, including his grandmother, had now turned against him. Kisemei once again found himself homeless. For a time, he found shelter at his church. He slept on the pews and washed in the river before he went to school each day, but he found no sustainable source of food, often filling his stomach with water to soothe the pangs of hunger. But even as he began to slowly starve, he continued to press on with his schooling.

One morning, however, weakness as a consequence of starvation was more than he could manage.

"Okay, class, line up," announced his teacher. It was customary for the students to stand in line for inspection before class.

As his teacher walked past each student, she caught a sudden rush of motion out of the corner of her eye. With a thud, Kisemei lay unconscious on the floor. His teacher and classmates rushed to his aid.

"Kisemei! Kisemei, wake up!"

Moaning, Kisemei opened his eyes and looked blankly around the crowded circle of concerned faces.

"Are you okay?" asked his teacher.

"What happened?" asked Kisemei.

"You fainted," explained his teacher. "Now tell me, is everything alright?"

Kisemei paused, sluggishly considering his circumstance, and then answered. "I could not stand because my stomach is empty, so I fell down."

"Someone find something for him to eat," said his teacher. "And Kisemei, you rest here for a while."

Only after Kisemei was given some food did his weakness subside enough to go inside for class.

After church one Sunday, a woman paid particular attention to one young man that she noticed had not left for home after the service.

"Hello, young man."

"Hello, ma'am."

"What is your name?"

"Kisemei, ma'am."

"Where are your parents?"

"They are not here. I come to church alone."

"Why are you still here? Aren't you going home? I noticed you last Sunday too. I did not see you leave last week either."

Then Kisemei told her what had happened to him. He told the woman that since becoming a Christian, his family had chased him away for breaking the rules of his culture.

Shyly he admitted, "So since then I have been living in the sanctuary."

With an austere look of worry, she took Kisemei's hand. "We must do something about this. Come with me. We will go talk to Mr. Noah."

Noah Leyiano was the pastor of the church. His congregation called him Mr. Noah. After hearing all the woman had to say, Mr. Noah invited Kisemei to stay in his home. "You are welcome to stay with us, but we do not have much."

Circumstances were just as his pastor had said. Even though this newfound hospitality afforded a more comfortable place to sleep, the pastor's family was quite poor, and often there was not enough food for everyone in the household. Kisemei stayed with the pastor's family until he completed the eighth grade. Hunger remained an ever-present part of his life during that time.

At school, Kisemei started an evening prayer group for students to pray together regularly. One evening as several students were praying, Kisemei heard a startlingly clear, powerful voice speaking directly to him. He later recalled, "It was distinctly separate from the voices of the students."

The voice said, "I have called you to the nations to be my voice, said the Lord."

Kisemei instinctively looked in the direction of the voice. Considering the clarity and volume of the words, he naturally expected to see someone standing quite close to him who had just spoken these words. But instead, he saw no one in that direction at all. That surprised him, and he began to feel a jolt of urgency as he contemplated what this could mean.

The following Sunday, Kisemei visited with his pastor about the experience, hoping to find some insight into its meaning.

"Pray to God. He will make it clear to you," his pastor said.

Days of prayer and Scripture reading turned into weeks, which turned into months. All the while, Kisemei continued to pray regularly for an answer to what the voice had meant. He felt a deep urge to share his faith and the salvation experience that had brought him to that point in his life. He became convinced that God was calling him into Christian ministry.

From then onward, Kisemei began to boldly share the good news of Christ with anyone he might encounter—strangers and schoolmates alike—along the village pathways, on the school campus, at the marketplace, and even going house to house, just as the missionaries who encountered him in his village had done less than a year before. Kisemei started an evangelism ministry at his school, and many students and teachers came to know Christ through his efforts. The number of converts to Christianity from this ministry was large enough that he helped form several Christian student unions in schools around the area. Around 400 children attended the weekly Wednesday evening Christian union fellowships. It was in the midst of this rush of evangelism that Kisemei began to preach, even though he was still in middle school. His ministry continued into high school where new Christians there would also form a Christian student union.

But even though he had been spared from death by his tribe, the price of following Christ remained painfully high for Kisemei. When his mother and his uncles heard that Kisemei had asked his pastor to come to his school to baptize a large number of students and teachers who had recently experienced salvation, they finally cut him off from their family entirely, believing he was lost.

You could argue that Kisemei had found himself orphan-like yet again, but this time was different. Although the pain of this rejection remained, Kisemei was not alone this time. He had found a new family—his brothers and sisters in Christ.

Like the others in his class, Kisemei sat for his annual exams at the end of his eighth-grade year. But unlike the exams from previous years, these tests carried more weight. They would determine whether he would qualify to pursue an education beyond the end of middle school. He was proud of the education he had worked so hard to achieve up to that point, and he wanted to press onward with his schooling after that year. Much to his delight, as a result of his exam scores, he was invited by letter to attend high school.

But high school was not mandatory in Kenya. If a student wanted to attend, there was a tuition fee. No longer supported by his family in any way, he knew he would have to try to pay for school on his own. But try as he may, he could not scrape together enough money to register for his high school classes. He approached his church to see if anyone in attendance in the congregation could help, but because the church and its members were very poor, they could not help him.

In desperation and as a last resort, he reached out to his uncles for help.

As he approached his village, one of his uncles called out to him. "Kisemei! What are you doing here? Go away. We do not want you here anymore. Go back to where you were."

"Uncle!' greeted Kisemei from a distance. "Let me talk to you."

"Oh, go away," moaned his uncle as Kisemei reached the house.

"Uncle, I need your help."

Reluctantly succumbing to curiosity, his uncle sighed, "What is it, boy?"

"My eighth-grade exam scores were good—good enough that I received this letter inviting me to go to high school." Kisemei produced a tattered envelope and thrust it toward his uncle.

Pursing his lips and slumping slightly, his uncle begrudgingly and slowly took hold of the envelope as he inhaled and exhaled deeply through his nose. He grasped the envelope limply, just enough to prevent it from falling.

As his uncle fumbled with the edges of the papers in the envelope, Kisemei continued. "But high school is not free."

His uncle rolled his eyes at Kisemei as he wrinkled his brow in disgust.

"And I know you do not want me here. But I cannot pay for school on my own. I have tried to find work, to earn a little money, but I do not have enough . . ."

"I will talk to my brothers," interrupted his uncle. "And I will tell your mother you were here, but for now, go away. I will discuss this matter with them. Come back later after we have thought about it."

In a few hours, Kisemei raised the courage to go back to hear their decision. When he returned to the house, he found several of his uncles there talking together.

"We have talked it over," one of his uncles told him flatly, "and we will pay for your school."

Kisemei gasped in gratitude as he began to smile slightly.

"And we will let you live here with us so you can walk to the nearby high school. We will feed you and give you clothes too."

Kisemei's surprise was beginning to give way to a sense of reserved celebration as his uncle spoke.

"But," his uncle thrust his index finger sharply upward as he glared wide-eyed into Kisemei's face, "to have this, you must abandon that stupid Christianity." They all looked on, waiting for a near-certain response of submission.

The young boy's hopes were frozen in disappointment once again as he paused and stared back at his uncles. After only a short moment, he gathered his answer.

"I think I had better miss what you are offering me than to miss my Christ."

Shocked and enraged, his uncles began to scold and shout at him as they demanded he leave, this time with a warning not to return.

With nowhere else to go, Kisemei retreated down the dusty road that led away from his village and made his way back to his church where he found his pastor.

"Pastor Noah, I do not know what to do. I want to keep going to school, but my family has abandoned me."

When Kisemei had finished retelling all the events that had recently transpired, Mr. Noah consoled the boy and resolutely responded, "Pray and fast for one week, and see what answers God has for you."

"I will, sir," Kisemei gratefully replied. "Thank you."

The following Friday was an uneventful day—uneventful until late that afternoon at around 4:00. It is a time that remains stamped in Kisemei's memory to this day because of the extraordinary moment that awaited him.

CHAPTER XIII

Provision

As Kisemei left the church compound to go for a walk that afternoon, he suddenly found himself face-to-face with one of the uncles who had thrown him out of his house only days before. Without a word of greeting, his uncle asked, "Have you seen your mother?"

"What?" asked Kisemei, perplexed.

"Have you seen your mother?" repeated his uncle.

Confused, Kisemei replied, "No. I don't know. Maybe she is at the market."

Shuffling impatiently, his uncle answered "No she isn't there. I cannot find her."

His uncle looked around the area impatiently for a moment and then explained. "Lately your mother has not been herself. She has been deeply troubled every night, unable to sleep enough and finding no peace during the day. She has this dream that keeps haunting her every night. And sometimes during the day, she leaves. This time I cannot find her. I thought maybe she was here with you."

"I have not seen her," Kisemei reported. Then pausing, he asked, "Uncle, what kind of dream does she have?"

"Every night she dreams that someone keeps calling her name, begging her . . ."

"Begging her for what?"

"Begging her to help you, Kisemei." Glancing around him again, the uncle continued. "Your God has touched the heart of your mother. I must help her. I will pay for your first semester of high school."

Surprised, Kisemei responded with instant elation. "Oh, thank you! Thank you so much!"

Just as quickly, though, Kisemei's enthusiasm fell. "Uncle, thank you, but it is already too late to sign up for the school I want."

"It doesn't matter," his uncle clarified. "Because you have disobeyed and have refused to renounce Christianity, I will not be bothered to pay for a well-performing school. I will send you to Kimana Secondary School. It is closer and cheaper. It will be good enough for you."

At first, Kisemei was disappointed by the lukewarm news. But as he prayed, he felt an answer come to him, saying, "I am sending you there to serve me."

Soon after classes began, circumstances confirmed to Kisemei that this was God's plan. Early on, he started a prayer group at his school. The group regularly prayed that God would save the students from the epidemic of alcoholism and drug addiction that plagued the school. Kisemei began to preach to the kids in his school. Within a month, every student in his class gave their life to Christ, except for one who was already a practicing Catholic. In all, 70 students became Christians at Kimana that first month. The school administrators appointed him chairman of the school's Christian Union. He served in that position for the next three years.

As his first semester of high school drew to a close, Kisemei knew the tuition funding his uncle had provided was coming to an end, just as he had promised. Kisemei was faced with the reality that he would soon, once again, be unable to attend school.

But just as classes were ending for the winter break, the principal learned that an anonymous donor wanted to sponsor bright Christian students from a Maasai background. The principal recommended Kisemei for this scholarship, and Kisemei's funding was secured for one more semester.

As Kisemei arrived to register for classes at the start of his second year of high school, his principal pulled him aside. "I need to speak to you."

"What is it, sir?" asked Kisemei.

"I . . . I don't know how to say this exactly, but . . ."

"But what, sir?"

"Kisemei, you have to trust God because your sponsorship has ended."

"So I can't go to school," concluded Kisemei.

His principal continued, "We don't know what will happen next semester, but just come to school. You have to trust God."

As the semester began, Kisemei arrived to attend as usual, trusting that somehow it would all work out. He arrived with nothing of his own, not even basic hygiene items. The students offered the contents of their lockers to him so he could use soap and other essentials as needed. It was under these circumstances that the school administrators allowed him to remain enrolled in school, cautiously optimistic that tuition funding would eventually arrive, although at the time funding remained unavailable.

Early in the semester, Kisemei was invited to preach at a Presbyterian youth conference in Nairobi. He decided to accept the invitation and resolved that he would have to walk there. At that time, he had no idea how to get to Nairobi, let alone that it was about 250 miles away. When he learned of the great distance he would have to travel, he decided he would have to take a bus. Two days before the conference was scheduled to begin, Kisemei packed a small bag with a few things and left on foot for the bus station without any money.

Watching the buses arrive and depart, he continued to sit on the bench at the roadside bus stop. Finally, he saw the passengers enter the last bus of the morning, watching solemnly as it drove away.

Late in the afternoon, the pastor's wife was surprised to see Kisemei walking through town. "I thought you left to go to the youth conference. Are you still going?" she asked. She had no idea that he had no money.

"Yes, ma'am. I am still going. In fact, I am on my way back to the bus stop."

Returning to the bus stop for a second time, Kisemei patiently waited and watched as once again each bus came and went until the final bus of the day departed. In the calm of the empty road, he felt the urge to linger for just a while longer. As he sat there, he saw a government Land Rover hastily approaching along the dusty road. Kisemei felt an intense compulsion to flag down the vehicle and sprang to his feet, waiving for the man to stop.

The vehicle slowed down, and the driver opened the door. "Yes?" asked the driver.

"Please, sir, I need to get to a conference in Nairobi today," explained Kisemei.

"Well, you are in luck. I just dropped off the district commissioner, and I am headed back to Nairobi now. I can give you a ride to the city, but you will have to find your own way to the conference."

Overwhelmed with gratitude, Kisemei climbed into the back seat, clutching his small bag. As they rode along, the driver repeatedly glanced in the rearview mirror at his strange passenger. He quietly listened with a degree of concern as Kisemei sat with tears freely flowing, sobbing an audible prayer, thanking God for providing transportation for him just in time.

When the driver stopped for food in Emali, he reached his arm along the top of the front seat and looked back at Kisemei. "Let me get you something to eat."

"I'm grateful, sir, but I have been fasting, explained Kisemei. "I do not think I can eat anything solid."

The driver went into a local shop and bought Kisemei a bowl of soup, which he gladly ate. As the driver watched Kisemei eat, he asked, "Exactly where in Nairobi is it that you are going?"

Kisemei showed the driver the address he had, and the driver offered to take him all the way to the conference, an offer Kisemei gladly accepted. But when the driver delivered Kisemei to the front door of the church that was hosting the conference, circumstances proved to be far from what Kisemei had anticipated.

CHAPTER XIV

Healing Faith

It was his local high school Christian union that had sent him to the conference and had taken care of the correspondence with the Presbyterian conference leaders. But when Kisemei arrived at the conference desk, his reception was much different than he had expected.

"May I help you, young man? Are you here for the youth conference?" The receptionist asked.

"Yes, ma'am."

"Okay. Your name, please?"

"Kisemei Kupe. I was invited to preach at the conference."

The woman lifted her finger from the roster of registered youth, looked up at Kisemei, and smiled. "I'm sorry, son. There must be some mistake. We did invite a Mr. Kisemei Kupe to preach, but he is much older than you. He's an elderly gentleman."

"But I have this letter of invitation."

The receptionist interrupted. "I'm sorry, young man. Obviously, there was a misunderstanding. We would be happy for you to attend, but we can't have you preach."

Learning that he had nowhere to spend the night, a widow who ran the church's mission center invited him to sleep at the center even though it had no beds available. But Kisemei was accustomed to many nights in similar circumstances. Although he slept on some sacks on the floor with his small bag for a pillow, he was grateful for the shelter.

The next day, Kisemei arrived at the conference as a student attendee. As a consolation for the previous day's confusion, he was offered a few minutes to speak. They told him, "You can share your testimony a little bit, but we can't let you preach."

After hearing the news, Kisemei became convinced that there must be a reason he was able to attend the conference after all. As he entered the crowded room, he silently prayed, "God, please cause a miracle within 15 minutes of this testimony I will share."

As he spoke at the conference that day, Kisemei felt that God touched his mouth and chose his words as he opened the Scripture and preached for the first five minutes. As he spoke, all those present started to kneel down one by one, some crying as they listened to his testimony and the Word of God. He later recalled, "The Holy Spirit moved, and people even began to speak in tongues in the church. I've found that sometimes when you minister out of pure knowledge, it does not have as much impact as when you allow the Lord to use you. When the anointing is upon you, it's that anointing that changes everything."

After the conference, some of Kisemei's new friends gave him a ride to the town of Rongoi outside of Nairobi to visit a fellow named Silvin Safari, a friend of his who was working at a church in that town. Safari was about Kisemei's age and a preacher from Tanzania who had been brought to Rongoi by sponsors so he could help run the church there.

Arriving unannounced, Safari was delightfully surprised to see his old friend Kisemei again and set about preparing arrangements for several days of outdoor preaching and worship. The pair spent the next four days preaching and worshipping with music and ministry in the open-air setting Safari had set up downtown. That Friday evening during the conclusion of the service while Kisemei was praying for the people present, someone brought a blind girl up to the front of the crowd and asked Kisemei to pray for her. By this point in the evening, Kisemei was admittedly tired from the long day's events, but he agreed to lay his hands on the girl nonetheless. Closing his eyes, he prayed for her as he laid his hands on her eyes. He then quickly concluded, "Be healed in Jesus's name" and then turned to greet everyone and leave for the night.

As he walked away, he began hearing a muffled commotion rustling among those still lingering at the gathering in the distance behind him. It gave way to swells of startled awe, shocked laughter, and humble celebration.

"Pastor!" someone called out as Kisemei turned to investigate. "The Lord has opened the eyes of that girl."

The girl's family members were supporters of Safari's church. Soon after the girl's healing, they told Safari, "Even before this happened to our cousin, the Lord had been speaking to us about Kisemei."

"What did God say to you?" Safari inquired.

"He said that Kisemei has a problem, but we do not know what it is. We do not know what this means. Do you?"

"No. Maybe you should ask him," Safari replied.

In the common social culture of Kenya, personal struggles are not usually discussed with friends. But undeterred, a few members of the girl's family went to ask Kisemei directly what was wrong.

"I'm fine," was all Kisemei replied with a smile.

Later they tried to ask Kisemei in a different way but achieved no new result. The repeated encounters with the family troubled Kisemei, so he asked God, "Tell me, what do you want me to say to them?" After searching, he felt that God told him to open up to the family about his life and his continuing struggle to find the funding and support to remain in school.

The following day, the family invited Kisemei to tea. As they all sat together, the father of the family pressed, "The Lord has given us a burden about your life, and we don't know how we can help you."

Kisemei reached into his pocket and pulled out an empty hand. "Because of this." He gestured that his hand was empty. "Because of this, I cannot go to school. My family will not support me because I am a Christian."

As he spoke, the father of the family lowered his head and began to cry. When Kisemei finished telling them about the tribulations he had endured and his quest to press on with God's will, the man looked up at Kisemei with reddened, tearful eyes and pledged, "As long as I have a job, you are going to school."

The following Monday, the man took Kisemei to Nairobi where he bought him clothes and shoes. Kisemei was even given several new business suits, the first he had ever worn. Returning Kisemei to class the next day, the man paid Kisemei's tuition for the semester and continued to pay thereafter until he graduated, also sending him checks regularly for spending money, which Kisemei would often use to help support other classmates in need. The man remained so committed to Kisemei that he even delayed his retirement to continue to provide for his young prodigy.

Kisemei remained committed to preaching. There was a recording of a Billy Graham Crusade that his local church showed the kids in Sunday school. Kisemei loved to listen to Rev. Graham preach, and he wanted to be like him. It was a call that he felt was more important than even finishing school, but his pastor, who had become his good friend and mentor, encouraged him to finish high school and said, "You can't be like Billy Graham if you don't go to school."

Kisemei graduated from high school in 1992. Debt-free with a bright future awaiting him, that year he committed his life to full-time Christian ministry.

CHAPTER XV

Humble Service

After high school, Kisemei moved back to the church campus grounds that had once sheltered him through many struggles. The church appointed him to head the youth ministry, which subsequently grew from 25 students to over 260 during Kisemei's time there.

A year later, Kisemei was ordained as an evangelist and became the director of missions at the church. Soon after, he was appointed to head the youth ministry programs in the region of the Maasai lands, which encompassed 51 local churches in Kajiado County. Within his first year in this position, Kisemei was instrumental in planting 21 churches in previously unreached areas of the Maasai area.

During a visit to the offices of the Free Pentecostal Fellowship in Kenya, Kisemei was introduced to Maud Anderson, a missionary from Sweden. She toured the churches in the Maasai region with Kisemei and was impressed with his church-planting efforts in that area. As they traveled between churches, Maud asked, "Kisemei, have you been to Bible college?"

Kisemei paused, surprised by the inquiry. "No, ma'am, I have not. I don't think my family would want me to go, and I am certain they would not pay for it. They do not approve of what I am doing."

"You are being called to go to Bible college. You must go." Maud smiled. "God has touched my heart about it. I will sponsor you."

One month later, Kisemei's pastor brought him the application forms for Karen Christian College in Nairobi. Kisemei was admitted, and with the help of Maud Anderson and additional funding from a missionary scholarship, he graduated three years later with an Associate's degree in Bible Theology.

During his time at college, Kisemei met Joyce Naiyeso, a member of the Kikuyu tribe. In the Maasai culture, marriages are prearranged. It is considered unacceptable to marry someone outside the tribe. Even so, the two fell in love and were married on August 17, 1996.

As Kisemei expected, his family disapproved of the union, but circumstances unfolded that later softened their hearts. During the summer of 1996, while Kisemei was still in college, a cholera epidemic nearly claimed his mother's life. Kisemei took time off to visit her. As she recovered, her heart softened toward her son's new wife, and she gave Kisemei the blessing of her approval that he so deeply desired.

It was soon after this experience that a sweeping transformation took hold in the hearts of Kisemei's family. They each began to experience individual circumstances that eventually led all of them—his mother, uncles, brothers, and even his father—to become Christians. The change was truly transformative. After a lifetime of neglect and rejection, Kisemei, for the first time in his life, was fully accepted by his family. Now they held him in the highest regard, viewing him as their family pastor.

A year after they were married, Joyce and Kisemei welcomed their first child into the world—a boy they named Finney.

After college, Kisemei and his young family moved back to his hometown village where he continued his ministry, serving as associate pastor at his church. He was elected Regional Secretary for Maasailand Churches. In that role, he returned to what he had been doing before college—traveling from church to church and preaching. He also later established several evangelical groups at various churches in the area.

Although his life had been difficult in many ways, the land of the Maasai was Kisemei's home. There, he and his family were very comfortable with their ministry, and they were proud of the fruits of their labor. Even so, Kisemei began to feel a calling that troubled him.

"Joyce," he told his wife, "I feel God calling me to leave this place. I feel like he is calling us to move our home and serve in other places. What do you think that means?"

"I do not know, but ask God to make it clear to you."

On January 7, 2000, a letter arrived for Kisemei from Nairobi.

"It is from the Kabiria Church," he said as his wife looked on. Kabiria was a community in Nairobi.

"What does it say?" she asked.

With careful solemnity, Kisemei studied the words before his reply. Glancing up at Joyce, he reported, "They want me to be their pastor."

"Oh, Kisemei!" she exclaimed, "What will you tell them?"

"This is our home," Kisemei gestured around him with his hands. "It would be very hard for me to say yes." His gaze lowered as he continued. "But I must do what is God's will. I still feel him calling us away from here."

After a moment to ponder, Kisemei decided what he would do. "I could hear from men," he said, "but I want to know what God wants me to do. I will go into the wilderness and fast until God gives me an answer."

The next day, Kisemei set out into the African bushlands alone. He eventually found shelter in a natural cave along a stone outcropping. There he began praying and listening. One night after about a week of prayer and fasting, he had a dream. In the dream, a voice spoke to him saying, "Do not be afraid. I am with you, and I will be with you in the new mission field. I will show you where to start, and I will tell you what to say and do for me."

When he awoke, he carefully considered these words. Wanting to be sure that the dream was not his own mind's concoction, he prayed that God would also speak to his wife as he set out for home.

When he arrived home, Joyce was waiting with bursting enthusiasm to tell her husband what she had experienced. "Tell me what happened during your prayers," she said.

Kisemei explained the dream he had and the message he heard.

Joyce's smile spread broadly across her face as she laughed. "Wow! God has done it again. I had the same message. God is sending us to Nairobi."

Kisemei contacted the denomination's Regional Overseer, Pastor Silas Baabu. He told Silas they had decided to accept the invitation for the pastorate in Kabiria.

CHAPTER XVI

The Long Road Onward

The first year of ministry in Nairobi was difficult for Kisemei and his family. The region of the Kabiria neighborhood was small and very poor, located on the outskirts of the city. The air carried the pervasive odor of soot from the countless open fires the people used in their homes nearby. Many of the people of the area were consumed with drug and alcohol abuse, and prostitution was rampant. At first, Kisemei went to Nairobi alone. He started with no congregation at all. Going from house to house, he gathered about 25 people to attend the newly-founded church. After a while, he brought his wife and two small children to join him. Silas stayed close by, helping them with the transition from a rural to an urban ministry setting, something that proved to be quite different from what they were accustomed to.

During those early years, provisions were sparse. The congregation of his fledgling church was very poor and could not afford to support a pastor and his family. Nevertheless, Kisemei and his family served with all their hearts, trusting God as they went. They pressed on with their ministry although hunger was a constant concern. More often than they would admit to those around them, they would all go to bed hungry, having eaten nothing at all during the day. Kisemei's monthly salary was the equivalent of about $60 US. The church gave what it could, but his family subsisted with few articles of clothing and minimal provisions for years.

As they struggled, Kisemei was reticent to tell his congregation or anyone else around him about his family's suffering.

"I'm preaching about a God who can do miracles," he told his wife, "And still my family is suffering. How can I preach that God provides when my own family is still going hungry?"

One particular day after their children had gone without breakfast and lunch yet again, it became clear that there would not be food for dinner once more. In desperation, that evening Kisemei decided to share his troubles with a friend, another minister in his church who was also a construction foreman. He hoped his friend could lend him some money for food, but his friend had no money to spare. The foreman's wife did offer Kisemei a meal, but he promptly declined the offer. *After all*, he thought, *how can I eat when my family is hungry?*

When he returned home, he found his wife visiting with their land-lady. The owner of the house did not know of their plight and yet gave them some rice and five liters of milk that night as a gesture of friendship. Kisemei and his family never forgot the kindness she showed that night and the way God used that moment to provide for them all.

The Kabiria region was named after a local witch doctor who came from a very elite family. The man's witch doctor practice was a very lucrative business that he used to control the people in the community through the leverage of superstition. People would come to him with their problems and desires, paying him with cows, goods, and money in exchange for access to his perceived powers. In turn, the witch doctor would bury charms under a customer's house—charms he had purchased in Mombasa—and conduct a ritual that he claimed would intervene in each situation.

With all the rampant drug use, alcoholism, and prostitution, and with a wealthy witch doctor overseeing it all, Kisemei felt there was a demon controlling the area. He took a small scoop of soil, wrapped it in paper, and brought it home with him. He and his wife prayed for the land for seven days. They prayed that God would expel the evil forces in the land and restore the people. Soon after, the Kenyan government became interested in the Kabiria region and began to sell off parcels for redevelopment. In the ensuing years, Kabiria underwent a gradual metamorphosis into a more suburban setting.

In 2001, Kisemei was elected Regional Secretary to oversee the 80 to 90 churches in the Nairobi area in his denomination. He was later called as pastor of the Free Pentecostal Fellowship Church in Nairobi, a congregation of about 620 at the time, with four associate pastors working with him. He served in that capacity for the next 16 years. In 2009, he was elected Deputy General Secretary of the entire Free Pentecostal Church organization in Kenya, a position he held for four years.

During this time, he felt God was calling him even farther away. A voice was telling him, "I will give you the nations." With permission from the church board of directors, he was given permission to start a youth service in English, which quickly cultivated his fluency in the language. It proved to be an endeavor that attracted youth from all over the region who were also interested in practicing English.

Within a few years, he was able to make short trips to preach in Tanzania, Uganda, Rwanda, Zimbabwe, Ethiopia, Botswana, Madagascar, France, Belgium, Norway, Denmark, and eventually the United States, speaking in churches and conferences as he went.

In 2014, Kisemei attended a wedding in Abilene, Texas, after preaching at a conference in Houston. In Abilene, he preached at a local church and toured the city. He was impressed with the postgraduate theology classes offered by a local Baptist college, Hardin-Simmons University. He met with administrators there to see if they would allow him to take some of the theology classes online from Kenya, but he was disappointed to learn that the university did not offer that particular course online. However, they encouraged him to apply for their postgraduate program anyway. He repeatedly asserted that he could not afford their tuition and would only attend if his entire family could be brought to the United States. The administrators encouraged him to pursue the opportunity anyway as they diligently worked to secure scholarship funding and the necessary visas.

In 2016, the opportunity to study in Texas came to pass. With funding in place and visas for himself, his wife, and every one of his children, they said goodbye to their friends and family and set out for the United States. While Kisemei was in class, Joyce took advantage of the opportunity to study at the local university to become a nurse. Their children enrolled in the local schools, making friends and also becoming involved in sports and the local church.

After completing his postgraduate degree in Texas, Kisemei and his family plan to return to Kenya to provide sound, theological, educational preparation for marginalized young preachers in that part of Africa. Kisemei's goal is to eventually open a training facility where he can provide short and efficient yet highly effective theology courses to students all over the Maasai land, fortifying the theological background of Christian students who cannot afford to attend college by allowing them to attend lectures and provide internship programs. He hopes to also encourage international students to volunteer their time and effort toward the fulfillment of this purpose.

After my last interview with Kisemei, he leaned forward with a gleam of vigorous determination, passionately gesturing as he spoke. "I have faith that local church ministry and teaching is the work to which God has called me. My heart throbs to spread the gospel."

Epilogue

Three years before Kisemei and his family traveled to America, Kisemei's father, Kupe Lenkujuk gave his life to Christ. It was transformative for Kupe, a man who had been consumed with alcohol addiction, a man who had caused so much pain, division, poverty, abuse, and neglect for his family and community. After his encounter with the Savior, Kupe became a testament to this saving power. He quit drinking and sought restoration and forgiveness from his family members. For the first time in his life, Kisemei was able to build a relationship with his father. In Kisemei's own words, "God restored my relationship with him."

One cool windy morning in March 2017, Kisemei was busy with his theological studies at Hardin-Simmons University in Abilene, Texas, when a message arrived from Kenya. When Kisemei heard the news, he said, "My whole world darkened with a black cloud. My father was no more. Tears rolled down my cheeks [because] before my father died, he gave a condition for his burial that it not be done without my presence." Kisemei was more than 8,000 miles from his home and his family on the other side of the world. Under the conditions of his temporary visa in the United States, no one in his family was permitted to work to earn money except for his own part-time university job that accompanied his coursework. "I was not able to raise [the money for] my airline ticket to go and bury him," remembered Kisemei. It seemed hopeless that he could honor his father's last wishes, so he gave instructions to his family in Kenya to begin preparations to bury his father without him.

Kisemei never forgot the moments of direct intervention in his past circumstances, all as a result of prayer. He once again sought the hand of divine intervention. Texting some of his fellow local church members, he asked for prayer. The senior pastor of his Texas church soon arrived at Kisemei's home to pray with him. The pastor reassured Kisemei that the church members would support him and find a way for him to fly back to Kenya for his father's burial. Within a matter of days, the money and provisions for the round-trip journey to Kenya were collected, the tickets were purchased, and Kisemei was on his way home to honor his father's final wish.

It is always hard at any age or in any circumstance to lose a parent. But for Kisemei, it was especially difficult because the consequences of the sins of his father had deprived them both of a lifetime together. "However, the comfort I had for my father's death was [that] he had given his life to Christ," Kisemei recalled.

Kisemei stayed in Kenya for a short time after the funeral to visit with friends and family before returning to Texas. It was during this time that he began to experience intense, unrelenting pain in his abdomen. The severity of his symptoms compelled him to seek medical attention at a nearby hospital. An ultrasound performed at the facility soon revealed that his gallbladder was severely inflamed—a condition called acute cholecystitis. The doctor informed him that the only effective treatment was to have his gallbladder surgically removed and that the surgery should be done very soon to prevent gallbladder rupture and the spread of infection or possibly even death.

As is the case in many countries around the world, the procedure would not be performed until Kisemei could produce the money for this expensive surgery. Kisemei knew he did not have the money for the procedure he needed. Believing in the power of prayer in numbers, he sent word to his friends and family in Kenya and in the United States to join him in prayer. But the money for the surgery did not arrive. As Kisemei lay ill in his bed for the next few days, he continued to pray, never giving up hope. He thanked God for all he had done for him in his life, and he asked for healing. One morning a few days after his diagnosis, he awoke to the realization that his pain was gone. The doctor knew it would be exceedingly rare for an inflamed gallbladder to heal on its own, so he performed a second ultrasound to see for himself. The doctor believed that the results of the ultrasound were undeniable. There in the images was a normal, healed gallbladder. Kisemei had fully recovered without surgery, and he was sent home from the hospital, cleared for the upcoming airline travel back to Texas.

One afternoon in early 2020 during the days of the COVID-19 pandemic, Kisemei and his family visited with my wife and me in his living room in Texas. He shared with me the latest set of uncertainties he was encountering. The university he was attending was closing its School of Theology due to financial hardships. For various reasons, Kisemei's family visas were in jeopardy of expiration, and it was very likely that they might have to leave the country before their educations in America were complete. Their oldest son had already been forced to return to Kenya just over a year before. We began to reminisce about the struggles each of us had encountered in the past. As we shared stories about the ways we had experienced God's intervening hand in those circumstances, Kisemei and his wife, Joyce, completed one another's sentences as they said something I will never forget.

"If you wait on the Lord, he will come for you. We know. We have seen it happen over and over again."

During the following months as the age of COVID-19 settled around the world, I was busy passing my spare time editing another draft version of this book when word arrived from Kisemei. He had applied for a position as a ministry coordinator at Hardin-Simmons University. Upon receipt of his application, the university eagerly placed him at the top of a short list of qualified candidates, and within a matter of weeks, Kisemei was hired. In his new position, he would serve an integral role in the Department of International Student Services and also as a liaison for students applying from Kenya. Circumstances rapidly fell into place after that, which secured the proper visa status for Kisemei and his family to remain in the United States and complete the remainder of their training and service.

Throughout their long and arduous journey in this world, Kisemei and his family have scarcely known the fleeting pleasures of material prosperity. Yet in all my days, rarely have I encountered anyone as wealthy as they are in Christ.

Joyce and Kisemei in traditional clothes from their clans

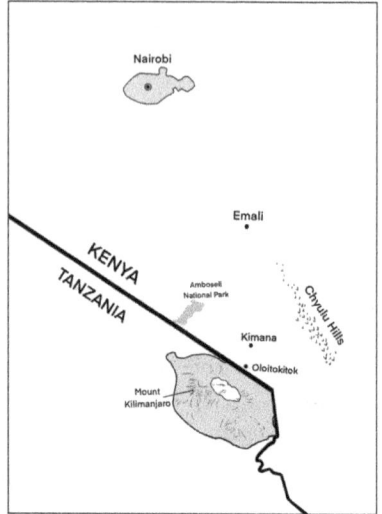

Map

Kisemei and his wife Joyce

Kisemei Preaching

Maasai village goat pen

Cattle on a Maasai Ranch near Kisemei's Village

Maasai Warriors and Moran

Kilamanjaro and elephants

Maasai with traditional house in background

Kisemei Leading Maasai in Prayer

More Maasai Warriors and Moran

Maasai village adobe huts